DREAMING
WITH OPEN
EYES

POEMS FOR VINCENT VAN GOGH

LOUIS
MARTINELLI

To Melissa —
with my best wishes
Louis Martinelli
5/20/2021

Up On Big Rock Poetry Series
SHIPWRECKT BOOKS PUBLISHING COMPANY
Minnesota

IN®
DIE

Cover Photo, Self-portrait (1887) by Vincent Van Gogh,
digitally enhanced by rawpixel.
Original from The Rijksmuseum, Amsterdam.
Cover & interior design by Shipwreckt Books
Published in Rushford, Minnesota

To Paul Gruchow, for your good ear.
To Teresa, for your good heart.

Dreaming with Open Eyes
Poems for Vincent Van Gogh

March 30, 1853

A day begins
In Southern Holland.
It is spring, the 19th century
Not yet tired of itself.
Joanna Van Gogh
Births a healthy child
Vincent Willem
Named for the lifeless brother
Stillborn on this day
One year ago—
Curse of replacement
Fate already weaving a future
From the irredeemable past.

Van Gogh Is Five Years Old

Clings to his mother's arm
As he bathes
Has bread and jam for breakfast
Wonders when father
Will be home from church
Tries to remember his prayers
Wanders aimlessly outside
Seeing everything.

Every Good and Perfect Gift

Comes down
From the father
Of heavenly lights

As snow came
To the Dutch moors
Filled the crotches

Of trees, covered
The frozen lakes
The windmills

No longer turning
Van Gogh silent
And sleeping.

The Light Wakes Van Gogh

But he does not paint it
Only wants to feel in his body
The God from which it came.

Van Gogh Speaks of His Technique

In the pattern of weaving
Overlay, underlay
I found my metier:
Cloth becoming paint
A woman's hands moving
The frame, thread joining thread,
A strange light come into the room.

Walking with Van Gogh

I followed him all over Holland
Briars and thorns covering
His wool coat. He never
Stopped talking—
Was this mania or just
The itinerant preacher
In love with the world—
We never paused
To look at anything.
I expected Van Gogh
To be observant like Thoreau
Sauntering across New England.

He ate very little
Drank too much
Cared nothing
About the blister
On my foot
Poked fun at my accent
Which he said
Reminded him of a voice
He'd heard in a dream
About a fog horn
Trying to break into his house.

The only thing I remember
Saying all day was
Vincent: it's a good damn thing
This country's flat.

Van Gogh Addresses the Blank Canvas

I don't care
How many times
You whisper to me
You cannot
Like a wronged lover
Seeking revenge
For some imagined affair.
I will have my way with you
Bold stroke by bold stroke.
I will cover you
With all the colors
Of my passion.
Were we not made
For each other?

To the Fields of Provence

Van Gogh carries his easel
His wooden perspective frame
His paint thick as glue
Sits down among laborers
And works
Good Protestant that he is.

In the Vineyard

Van Gogh climbs
A trellis
Hears the voice
Of Jacob

Wrestles an angel
In love with
His blue eyes
And auburn hair.

Sometimes a Divine Sadness

Fills me, Van Gogh wrote,
Perhaps thinking of the stillborn
    brother
For whom he was named
Or the fragile earth he loved.
In the flower paintings
Color overwhelms melancholy
Perspective is replaced
By an almost microscopic
Attention to detail
As if the artist were inviting us
To touch the bold strokes
To smell the oils he has labored
To mix and layer
To accept these gifts he has
Received from nature
Consolation for being mortal.

Emily Dickinson Muses on Van Gogh

Take away the madness
His life becomes a room—
Tulip, iris, rosemary
A place for hope to bloom.

Take away the sadness
There's nothing left to feel—
The sun's already shown defect
That time shan't ever heal.

Take away the paintings
The world shrinks like a death—
Inventors cannot recreate
The work of God's own breath.

Samuel Becket Writes to Van Gogh

Fear nothing
Except certainty.

Commit the heresy
Of self-love.

Make art
From desperation.

In the next life
Shun fame.

Van Gogh Finds His One True Love

Nothing good lasts:
He knows this. The
Provencal sun shines
Down on a canvas
Already layered, ready
For these once-in-a-century
Hands to begin again.
On this day, Van Gogh will
Make the brush strokes
With so much tenderness
So much love
For the Cypress tree
And the sun, the grass
Growing under his feet
It will be as if the painting
Is alive
And he is married to it.

After Seeing the Harvest by Cezanne

Van Gogh draws, then paints
The first of eleven sowers.

Wanting to express
"His longing
 For the infinite"
He depicts a violet field
The sky and sun
A deep yellow
The ripe wheat chrome.

The man who is sowing—
Nearly indistinguishable
From the plowed field—
Looks tired but content
His right arm
Swinging at his side
Like a branch in the wind
His left hand inexplicably
Grasping his chest.

Perhaps his most
Prophetic work
Van Gogh announces here
That he is a missionary
Evangelizing an art
Of the future—
Consolation for a world
In which machines
Will remove men from
The place of their labor.

Van Gogh's Lover Sien Hoornik Writes to Him

You've gone home
As I knew you would
I forgive this abandonment
As I've forgiven
All the others.
When the children ask
If you are returning
I tell them I don't know.

I will always be grateful
For your kind heart
For feeding us
And for the drawing of me
On which you printed
The word "Sorrow."

Van Gogh Answers Sien Hoornik

Your letter broke what is left
Of my shameful heart.

Father has forbidden me
From marrying you

Threatening to commit me
To an asylum for the insane.

I pray for the children
And for you.

How can it be
A woman such as you
Is alone in this world?

I am once again
Living in the family parsonage
Sleeping and eating better

Painting a little
Studying with Mauve
At the Hague.

I believe the drawing of you
I called "Sorrow"
Is my best work.

Sorrow

Her breasts hang like gourds
On withered vines
Her face hidden
By two despairing arms
Her fingers and toes long
Her hips small for a woman
Who is several months pregnant.

Long, stringy hair
Falls over her shoulders
Like a shredded, wool cape.

In Paris Van Gogh Discovers Opera

Falls in love
With the colors
Of the human voice
Especially the Italian
Of Puccini
Identifying not so much
With Rudolfo
The grandiose poet
In La Boheme
But with self-effacing Mimi
Whose tragic flaw
Was to love beauty
More than food.

Van Gogh Writes to All the Painters Who Have Ever Lived

I've noticed something
About the women's faces
In your work—
They're all the same—
Greek, Italian or
From some other planet
The eyebrows arched
The perfect nose
Lips thin, symmetrical
And almost always
Without emotion.
I have to tell you
Something I've kept
Secret all these years:
This is a woman
I've never met.

In the Seventeenth Century

A mini ice age appeared
Deepening winter in Holland
Keeping the swamps and lakes
Frozen well into spring.
When snow fell in summer
Nature appeared hostile
Artists turned inward
Time stood still as it does
In a pandemic
When each day comes
To feel like every other.
Johannes Vermeer captures
This moment in environmental
History, working in pigments
Covered by transparent glazes
Freezing movement itself
In domestic scenes
Most famously The Milkmaid.
When the earth warmed again
The energy that moves the sun
Transformed painting,
Van Gogh freeing
Paint itself from its prison.

Van Gogh Turns East

And learns to see—
The 19th Century Japanese master
Hiroshige guiding him
Across bridges and mountains
And rivers that make of the visible world
A place of delight, a heaven,
So that 5,400 prints later
Van Gogh understands what
Hokusai the woodcut artist
Meant when he said of his own work
"It is only pictures of the floating world
Through which I pass like a small leaf."

In Van Gogh's Starry Night Over the Rhone

The river is shining
Lit by stars the size
Of the sun
And by what appear
To be pagodas
With large masks
On the outside.
The night sky
The water
The earth
Are shades of blue
Which grow darker
The farther we look.
A man and woman
Dressed for winter
In heavy coats and scarves
Are walking away
From the yellow lights.
Unlike the figures
In Van Gogh's
"Undergrowth with Trees"
There is no despair
On their faces
Which have human features
And appear to be happy
As the man and woman
Turn to walk home
Still in love, still in awe
Of this miraculous universe.

Today Van Gogh Is Thirty-Two

The sky gives only rain
And not inspiration
His lover and her children
A distant memory
His father dying
His own body
Full of venereal disease.

He lives by
The benevolence
Of his family—
Another name
For failure.

But soon Van Gogh
Will begin painting
The Potato Eaters—
His most consuming work—
For two months
He will transform
Light into darkness
And darkness back
Into light
As five hungry peasants
Gather at table
Their simple meal
The last supper of Christ.

Skull with Burning Cigarette

In 1885 Van Gogh's father dies
The Catholic priest in Nouen
Forbids villagers
To sit for Van Gogh portraits
And in what might be
His first self portrayal
Paints a skeleton
Smoking a cigarette
Mocking the drawing class
In which he is forced
To copy anatomical lifelessness
A hint of self-rebuke
In the subtle, unflattering reflection
Of his own sunken face.

Soon Van Gogh
Will move to Paris
Grow closer to Theo
Make over 200 pictures
And learn the dead
Not only smoke
But can dance.

Self Portrait Dedicated to Charles Laval, December 1888

Having failed at six professions
And every relationship
Tired of reading Psalms
And waiting on the Lord
Van Gogh paints himself
As a twentieth century man
His face more handsome
Than any photograph shows—
Charlton Heston playing Jesus—
The chiseled features
And dark green eyes
Dignifying his pain
A lock of hair prophetically
Cutting across his ear.

In the next two years
Van Gogh will paint himself
Several times
But never again
Will he reveal the fierceness
That made him beautiful.

Van Gogh Keeps Dreaming He Is Lost

In someone else's dream—
Theo's or Gauguin's or his father's—
And he cannot wake up.

There is too much water
In these dreams—
The dykes cannot hold it back.

Van Gogh is afraid
He will drown
Before the boat arrives

With dry clothes
And his mother.

Van Gogh Hears the Sound Of the Double Helix

Before it was discovered by scientists
As hypothesis and formulae.
He is not surprised
To learn there is music
Playing inside his brain:
Once he heard
His grandfather's voice
At the graveside in Holland
When he knelt in homage
To the mystery of death.
Another time in Provence
He heard his own cells calling
To a flock of migrating birds.

Van Gogh, Delusional

Believes the poor
In their hunger
Are God

And he is feeding them
The fish of his painting
The bread of his hands.

Homeless, Unable to Work

Van Gogh sleeps under a bridge
On the road to Arles
A small fire at his feet
The stubble on his face
Growing thicker.

On this starless night
The other transients
Will give more warmth
Than his wet clothes
Or the struggling flame.

Van Gogh's Ear

Scorned for visiting brothels
Having sold only one painting
In his lifetime
Failure growing inside
Like a tumor
Van Gogh cuts off his ear
And gives it to Rachel—
A prostitute
At the House of Tolerance.

She puts it to her ear—
A sea shell
Covered with blood—
Hears the wind blowing
Through olive trees
The scraping of a knife
In a kitchen
And three crows
Flying across Provence.

I Dream Van Gogh's Ear Is Orbiting the Earth

Illegally—
The snail of the inner ear
The cochlea
Sending out waves
Of B-flat harmony
The tympanic membrane
Of the drum
Played by a circle
Of men
Who don't frighten
Children
Will not make war
On anyone.

Van Gogh Cries Himself to Sleep

For no reason
The voices come again
And shout: failure!

No matter the day's
Good work
Or the perfect symmetry
Of a leaf
Or Rachel baring
Her breasts.

It hurts to be mad
And on this night
Van Gogh weeps
Like a lost child.

Van Gogh Writes of Doctor Gachet

That he seems eccentric
But that his experience
As a mental doctor
Must keep him balanced enough
To combat the nervous trouble
From which he seems to be suffering
At least as much as me.

Up until now
I have done no one
Any harm. Is it
Fair to have me
Accompanied everywhere
Like a dangerous beast?

Doctor Gachet
Releases Van Gogh
From his prison
Knowing the painter
Will risk his life
For his work.

Letter From A Madman

There are moments
When the passion
Grows intense

Perhaps to the edge
Of insanity
Or vision

When I feel
Like the Greek oracle
On her tripod.

It is then
Color begins to speak
In tongues

Sound becomes
Many shades
Of green

And if we take
The train
To Rouen

We take death
To reach
A star.

In the Secret Annex

Anne Frank reads
Van Gogh's letters to Theo
Is moved by their eloquence
Desperation and tenderness
Remembers the narrow streets
And painted houses of Amsterdam
The museum where she learned
A new language of line, shape, color
Opens her diary and writes
"In their hearts people are good."

Letter to Van Gogh In Despair

Indulge me
For I have lost too many and too much
To expect a better end than you.
Still, I would turn away from pain
To praise the emptiness
From which the universe was made
The oven in which bread rises
The earth which makes of our broken hearts
Fleur-de-lis, tulips, roses
Rain which costs nothing
The farmer's strong hands
The weaver's thread.

After Trying to Distance Himself from Religion Van Gogh Paints Jesus Christ Without a Halo

More human than divine
This Christ in death
Is meek and humble
His limp shape
Conforming
To the granite floor
Of a cave
The grieving Mary
Opening her arms
As he falls to earth
Fulfilling the Gnostic
Prophecy.

But he is muscular too
The arms and shoulders
And large hands
Sculpted
As if he had done
Hard labor
The face, beard
And hair
A rusty tone
The eyes and nose
Resembling Van Gogh's
Own strong features.

Ostensibly a copy
Of Delacroix's

Monochromatic "Pieta"
Van Gogh
Describes the two heads
As "one somber-hued
And one pale flower"
And says he is an
Instrumentalist
Interpreting the work
Of a great composer.
The previous July
He had experienced
His worst attack
The world turned
Inside out—
And now in September
He has created
A Christ to comfort
The afflicted.

In the Thirty-Sixth Year of His Life

Van Gogh drew a man and woman
Walking through a field of sunflowers
Painted his own shoes
And sunflower heads in pairs
Which appear to have fallen
From their stalks
Onto a frozen blue lake.

There are also still lives
Of cut sunflowers
Which resemble miniature suns
Brought indoors for a banquet.

The Sunflower

The sunflower stands
For everything that bows
To earth
Its dark seed burning
Unrepentant as fire.

Van Gogh Dreams

He is drowning in paint
And no one can save him
Not Gauguin or Theo
Or Dr. Gachet
Although they try
Wading into a sea
Of color.

Flailing his arms and legs
The oil coating him
Like a seal
Van Gogh stops resisting
And walks on water
Blessing the fisherman
Who catches no fish
And the fisherman's wife
Waiting all night
In a starless field.

Van Gogh Ponders A Fatal Flaw in The Political Philosophy Of Machiavelli

If self-interest were all
Why does the sun go on
Burning itself out?

Van Gogh Accepts an Invitation from American Golf Prodigy Tiger Woods

Irreverent as ever
Van Gogh turns his hat sideways
Loads his bag with French bread and brie
Asks Tiger if he paints
Holds his club like a brush
Manages to take fewer strokes
Than any golfer in history
By refusing to play.

The Poet Jimenez Advises Van Gogh

If they give you ruled paper
Write the other way.

Van Gogh Decides To Write Fiction

But the words cling
To his wool coat
Like briars
The periods, commas
Semicolons
Walk out of the room
Unhappy to be
Subsumed in the
Vineyard of the text
The characters
Won't speak to each
    other
Until they know
How the story ends
And Van Gogh
Realizing he's opened
Pandora's box
Decides to paint
A pair of old shoes
With worn leather soles
Saving art from abstraction
While the novel
Begins to die
Its long, slow death
Its characters turning
Into talking machines
Who repeat, endlessly,
The same thing.

The American Humorist Garrison Keillor Finds Van Gogh Lacks Certain Musical Abilities

Fee, fi, fo, fum
Van Gogh couldn't play
The accordion.

Van Gogh Writes to Shakespeare's Wife

I feel toward you a tenderness
I've never felt
Toward any living woman.
Eight years your husband's senior
A country girl
Who herded cows, fed your lamb,
Practiced the arts of cooking, knitting,
Understood the courtship sonnets
Written to gain your favor
It puzzles me
How you've disappeared
Like a photograph in a fire
Even your ashes reviled.
But then, you're in such company:
Those wives of great men of letters—
Who nursed children
In empty marriage beds
As husbands prowled the world
In search of love, fame, inspiration.
I think we could have been happy, Anne:
After all, I didn't get along with men
Or make an art that causes kings to swoon.
My crimes were failure and insanity.
Yours being born too late and too soon.

Michelangelo Writes to Van Gogh
From Limbo

I've been here three centuries
Suspended by ropes
Painting heaven for those
Like me
Not yet ready for their
Eternal reward. Who knows
When that will be?
I did this once before
In Rome—
Some would say
My best work was accomplished
Lying on my back.
Its no miracle to embody
What one sees—
Though we sleep in darkness
Our dreams are lit by stars
As you well know.
How I long to stand
Next to you
In a field of wheat—
To call you brother
Break bread, drink wine,
And paint whatever
That day brings.

Van Gogh Writes to Michelangelo Bonarroti

You were married
To stone
I to canvas and paint—
Wives who were
Too much for us
Kept us awake
At night, struggling
To keep beauty alive
In the world.
What we made with
Our two hands
Became our children.
Like you, I worked alone
A slave to art's perfection
While our bodies—
Poor aging vessels
Holding two souls on fire—
Cracked and fell apart.
How I wish I'd known you
When I lived
In the yellow house in Arles—
I might have learned
From you
How to live and die
More gracefully.

Beauty

We make love
In the dark
Because the body
Will turn blue one day
Be pumped dry
Filled with chemicals
Or burned to ash
Gravity will take
Its most seductive
Features
And hang them
Like gourds
Like twisted vines
Even the burls of trees
Will be more comely
Than the furrowed skin
That was once
Smooth as satin.
In the dark womb
Of his mother
Van Gogh
Was already dreaming
With open eyes
And in the light
Thirty-six years later
He would lie down
In an olive grove
Because he said
Like the body of a woman
It was too beautiful
To imagine or paint.

At the Party for Van Gogh

After the toasts offered
With French wine
The brie and other cheeses
Devoured -
One can only wonder
How much Vincent would
Have stuffed in his
Wool pockets -
After the music
Played by two young
Prodigies
Wafted out into the street -
After I read my poems
To applause
And good questions
About the painter
Who changed the way
We see the world
Who gave his life
So that beauty might
Save us
I wanted only to sleep
With my beloved
Enclosed by
The holy silence that
Had found us again
Had healed the torn place
Where we were too long
In another life, then this one,
Apart.

The Dead Brother I

Stillborn
Frozen in time
Beautiful
As a death mask.

The Dead Brother II

In all the still life paintings
We are drawn into the scene
As witness to a strange disorder—
The fruit is mushy
The shoes worn
With nails visible
The iris in its vase
Grows in several directions—
As if Van Gogh
Were making room
For the dead one to live again
In the fate of the world.

Undergrowth with Two Figures
for Per Knutas

Only weeks before
Bad family genes and
Syphilitic spirochetes
Destroy most of
What remains
Of his sanity—
A broken heart
And the inability to
Earn a living
Doing the rest—
Van Gogh paints
Another masterpiece:
A faceless couple
Imprisoned within
Lilac Poplar trees
Strangely cobalt blue
Enough light
Penetrating the
Dense forest
To show pink, white
And yellow flowers
The tall grass
A luxurious green.
In his 896th letter to Theo
Van Gogh describes
This intimation of his end—
An imprisonment not
In the asylum
But in the God of nature
That he loved

Then says he has
Despaired of ever
Being married
As the faceless man
And woman
Lost in these woods
Seem to have despaired
As they wait to be found
Or to consummate
Their love in another life.

The Museum Technician Restores Undergrowth with Two Figures

The painting looks small
Outside its elaborate frame
Lying on a table like a corpse.
The technician works deliberately
Scraping thirty five years of wax
Off the one hundred twenty
Year old painting—
One of Van Gogh's last.
He explains how this
Will brighten the colors
Revealing more texture
In the trees, how there was
No protective varnish on
The surface of this masterpiece
How Theo and his wife Johanna
Left it alone.
Underneath his microscope
The brush strokes separate as if
They were strands of thread
In a woven cloth.
We are standing
Only a few feet from
This man who works so carefully
He could be a surgeon
Saving someone's life.
Looking down from this perspective
I see how the two almost faceless people
A man and a woman
Are not trapped in the forest
As if held against their will

But have given their lives
Like Van Gogh
To the flowers and the trees.

On Nine Eleven Eleven

The tenth anniversary
Of America's suicide bombing
By terrorists who killed 3,000
Innocent people
Leaving one more hole
Filled with blood in the world
I flee a one-sided football game
In which my team
Is being humiliated
Drive a few miles
To the art museum
Where Van Gogh's painting,
Two Figures In Undergrowth,
Has been restored
To its original brilliance—
Bright cobalt and mauve trees
White and yellow flowers
A man and woman, faceless,
Trapped within the forest
I think ominously as those
Poor souls who could not escape
The twisted steel and concrete
Of the Twin Towers in New York
On that day when Dante's Inferno
Seems, now, to have been almost
A comedy. No one checks
Me for bombs, or even a camera
At the museum entrance
But on this sunny day
There's a heaviness in the air
As I learn the Van Gogh will soon

Be reframed, more simply,
As he would have done it
Will be hung on a new wall
In a larger, brighter room.
When I find the blank space
Waiting for its masterpiece
I remember how an artist
Once came to see this painting
And touched it
In violation, of course, of
Museum rules, how she was
Escorted outside for this transgression
Van Gogh himself would have approved.
Today, no one ojects as
I draw with my hand
The obliterated Twin Towers
Back into existence
Here on the art museum's
Blank wall, adding people
Floor by floor, desk by desk—
Fathers, Mothers, Sons and Daughters
Spouses, Soulmates, Enemies, Friends—
Until the white space is full.

September 11, 2011

Interview with Van Gogh

What's the most important thing to you?
My hands. My feet.

What are you most proud of?
That I lived 37 years.

When did you make your first appearance?
In the asylum at St. Remy.

Who did you learn your style from?
Jesus

What are you most afraid of?
Success

What do you most want?
Success

Van Gogh Speaks of the Growing Distance Between Rich and Poor

The rich have found a way, finally,
To bypass the eye of the needle
By sewing it shut.

Van Gogh Speaks of His Last Love Affair

While visiting the stream
Where we were born again
In the first year of our new life
Two bluebirds sat on a tree
Silent as the day and beautiful
As if a piece of the sky
Had broken off and come down.
They were light in our hearts
Which were transported by love
And by the miracle of this day—
A couple themselves in love
With this place,
And happy to be with each other
To do no harm in the world
To give what they've been given
This light, this peace which
Surpasses all understanding.

What Would Van Gogh Do

If Jesus came a second time
Moving into the yellow house
In Arles, sitting down to supper,
Blessing Van Gogh's dream
Of a studio in the south
Where art could flourish
Like the miraculous loaves
And fishes?

All would be well
As Van Gogh grows old
No need for Theo's charity
Or the escape
From depression drunkenness
And self-mortification provide
Forgiveness freeing him
From the web
Three jealous sisters weave
Whenever genius comes
Into the world.

Gaugin, in Limbo, Remembers Van Gogh

I'm still not sure
Who you were
Or what it all means.
I've lost no respect
For you, Vincent,
Though we are
So different still
Time healing
None of our wounds.
I believed you mad
But here where
God is only a rumor
And there is no death
How I miss those
Nights in Provence
When the sky
Was filled with stars.

Salvador Dali Writes to Van Gogh
from the Middle of Nowhere

Listen to me Van Gogh:
I am Dali
The greatest surrealist
Painter of all time, of that
Iconic upside down
Christ on the cross
My wife Gaia the model -
And of the last supper
A beautiful image
For which I was handsomely
Rewarded by believers
And lovers of bad art
Until everything began
To dissolve -
My paints ran on the canvas
Like rhinoceroses fleeing
A hunter
My wife fell in love
With Judas
My sanity slipping away
Like yours
Until there was only
My beautiful black cane
And no more Dali.

Cezanne Writes to Van Gogh

You cared little for my modern methods;
I thought yours unruly and old fashioned.

But now I see in every rock
Tree and mountain

How we are brothers
Made invisible by the world we love

Nature erasing us
Until there is only Provence.

Van Gogh Walks A Labyrinth in Winter

I move in circles
Snow blinding me
The stone passageway
Buried under ten thousand flakes.

I don't know where I am
How far it is to the center.
If there is a God
I've not found her here.

Van Gogh Writes to Thomas Kincaid

You sold your soul
To sell a hundred thousand
   paintings.
I refused and sold only one.
They called you the painter
   of kitsch
Me the painter of paint
A madman who cut off
   his ear.
We both drank too much
The truth, perhaps,
Too hard to bear
No matter if it leads
To failure or success.
I want to take you
In my arms, Thomas,
And save you from
Your fate, give you back
The soul the world
Confused, oppressed.
A century has passed
And they still don't know
Who made the fatal wound
In my broken hearted chest.

His Mind Growing Dim

Van Gogh is drawn to light
Paints Crows Over A Cornfield
An explosion of yellow and blue
As if the painter had seen
The sun falling into an ocean.

Migrating crows
Struggle against wind
The prairie surrounding Auvers
The Garden of Eden
Turned upside down.

It is July, 1890—
The last year
Of Van Gogh's life.
Recent paintings
Show the effects
Of a capricious wind
As Dr. Gachet
Then the church at Auvers
Quiver and billow.

Van Gogh misses the North
His dream of fatherhood
His family
And imagines he is a bird
With great wings.

If We Were There

With you Vincent
In that room
Where you wrestle
Exhausted
With depression's inertia
Numb or in too much pain

Turning away from food
Not wanting to feed
The monster who lives
In your brain

We would cook for you
Filling the yellow house
With sweet basil
Barley and thyme.

Roulin

The Postman of Arles
Helped Van Gogh understand
The color blue – how deep
It was, how you could
Swim in it forever, like the sea.
In that final year, he
Companioned his friend
Through illness and grief,
Visiting him in the asylum
Bringing his mail.
His heart broken, he helped
Carry Van Gogh's coffin
To the grave, as if he were
Carrying a satchel
Heavy with the unbearable
Weight of a great soul.

Van Gogh's Prayer

Let me live long
In love with a woman's breast
The roots of Cypress
The sun.

Let my ears open
To whatever music comes
My hands refrain
From telling lies
My mouth refuse
To curse
The author of my pain.

Let me die a little mad
And not too vain.

At Van Gogh's Funeral

The mourners are so overcome
By shock and grief
They struggle to carry his body
To the grave. Theo, Dr. Gachet,
Roulin the postman
Are sobbing, their tears
Staining the wood coffin
With salt, their voices croaking
As they pay tribute to their
Brother and friend—
This man who gave his life
So we might believe, even now,
There is a soul breathing
Within the broken heart
Of this world.

Van Gogh Meets Rembrandt In Heaven

Because its never too late
To live happily ever after
You embraced me here
As if I were your prodigal son.
Together, we walked
Into the temple where
Jesus was preaching
Then followed him all
The way to the cross
Where you dressed in blue
Kissed the lifeless hand
Then painted
A resurrection in which
Jesus appears to Mary Magdalene
As lovers appear to each other
In dreams. You waited for me
Here, two hundred years.
I learned from you how
To see through a glass darkly—
How much light there is
In the face of God.

Elegy For Van Gogh

This man who fell to earth
And drank its water—
Who found another world
In this one, more brilliant
Than the sun—
Who raised God
From the dead
With paint and brushes—
Who preached a gospel
Of bad news
Of infinite grief

Whose heart was a river
Whose hands were light

May he rest
Under the drooping heads
Of sunflowers

May he fill
The black hole of history
With sight.

The Morning After

Holland loses its greatest painter
A cross shaped windmill
Creaks and groans
Under a sullen sky.
Its stone foundation—
The work of forgotten artisans—
Will last centuries
So carefully
Have the blocks been placed.
Inside, the grinding goes on all day
While somewhere a peasant works
In a field of wheat
Stops to curse the sun
Prays for his wife and child
Waiting at home.
He has never heard of Van Gogh
Who painted him in early October
One year ago
In the same place where
He, this new day beginning,
Is dreaming with open eyes
Of the earth's beauty
And of all he would give, now,
For a loaf of bread.

Van Gogh's Last Room

In Auvers is as he left it—
Austere and simple
A monk's hermitage
With one bed, one table,
A skylight which
Causes shadows to criss cross
In the emptiness
A calm to which
He returned each day
To eat a peasant's supper
Then dream of golden fields
Where ripening wheat
And crows flying overhead
Were waiting for him.

Afterword

"The only riches, the great souls."
D.H. Lawrence

It is a challenge to write prose about Vincent Van Gogh's life and work after spending fourteen years writing poems about him. I have come to know this amazing artist primarily through imagination, image, metaphor, and voice—the stuff of poetry. I'm not an art historian, or painter, so my understanding of Van Gogh grew as the poems grew. It was a humbling experience and I can only hope I've done Vincent the person and Van Gogh the artist some small justice. Van Gogh's own words often guided me; his letters are wonderfully written and reveal much about the person and his art. I reference them in my poems and quote them in the Afterword.

My interest in Van Gogh began in the year 2000 when I had the opportunity to view the Chicago Art

Young Vincent Van Gogh

Institute *Studio of The South* exhibit, which explored how Van Gogh and Paul Gauguin influenced each other's art. I found the exhibit a little overwhelming—from the crowded rooms to the sheer number of paintings and drawings—and I came away somewhat skeptical about the role Gauguin played in Van Gogh's work. More important for me was the two artists' vision of creating a studio in the South of France, where painters could work side by side, supporting and learning from each other in a creative commune.

When this dream failed to become reality, in part because the two men had incompatible personalities and diverging philosophies of art, the impact on Van Gogh seems to have been deeper than on Gauguin, who simply moved on. Van Gogh stayed put in his yellow house in Arles, France, and produced what many consider his best work. This final period of Van Gogh's life began, violently, when he cut off his ear after an argument with Gauguin, and ended with his death, which most historians attribute to suicide.

In those few years Van Gogh made a staggering number of paintings, many of which inspired poems in *Dreaming with Open Eyes*. Between paintings, he suffered from venereal disease and periods of mental distress—some of which resulted in hospitalization. Loneliness, anxiety, poverty, an increasing sense of alienation from his family in Holland, and a profound sense of failure plagued him. The number of paintings sold in his 37-year life—one painting— is perhaps the single most shocking fact in the history of art.

I'm not a historian or economist, so I doubt I can add much to the cliché that says artists like Van Gogh are ahead of their time. Some art historians have argued that he is the first truly modern painter, and it seems painfully obvious to anyone who has read his letters he is not in any sense a self-promoter, relying mainly on his brother Theo to exhibit and sell his work. The Van Gogh I discovered in writing poems about him seems to be an artist to whom craft mattered, and one whose vision was essentially spiritual, though not conventionally religious. I can't think of another Nineteenth Century painter who turned to weavers for his technique of layering on paint, nor can I think of one who sees so clearly the relationship between the everyday and the sacred.

While Van Gogh's paintings of peasant laborers are influenced by and resemble Millet's, Van Gogh seems to find something beyond the ordinary in these figures, and in the places where they worked. His use of color in his depiction of Roulin, *The Postman*, is one example of this ennobling effect, his painting *The Sower* another. This can only come from an intensity of feeling that colors the work, coupled with attention to craft. I kept finding what seems to be a search for the sacredness of everyday life in his work, perhaps having its roots in his Calvinist Protestant Minister father and in Vincent's own failed attempt to become a preacher in the Borage mining region of Belgium.

In 1884, in a letter to Theo, he wrote: "I am painting a loom of old, greenish, browned oak, in which the date 1730 is cut. Near that loom, before a

Drawing of Weaver and Loom

little window which looks out on a green plot, stands
a baby-chair, and a baby in it sits looking for hours at
the flying to and fro of the shuttle. I have painted the
thing exactly as it was in nature, the loom with the
little weaver, the little window, and the baby-chair, in
the miserable little room, with the clay floor."

Nine years before, in a letter to Theo from Paris
dated September 17, 1875, Van Gogh wrote: "A
feeling, even a keen one for the beauties of Nature,
is not the same as a religious feeling, though I think
these two stand in close relation to one another.

"Almost everybody has a feeling for nature, one
more, the other less, but there are few who feel God
is a spirit and whoever worships him must worship
Him in spirit and in truth. Our parents belong to
those few.

"You know that there is written: 'This world passes and all its magnificence.' And that there is on the contrary also mentioned a good part that shall not be taken from us, and 'a well springing up into everlasting life'. Let us also pray that we become rich in God …

"Let us ask that our part in life should be to become poor in the kingdom of God, God's servants. We are still far from it; let us pray that our eye may become single and that our whole body shall be full of light."

I think the progression of Van Gogh's paintings, during and after these important nine years, show how this inner light guided him—how he came to celebrate it and find it everywhere—in his ecstatic

The Starry Night

Drawing of Owl

rendering of an exploding universe in Starry Night to his simple, realistic drawing of an owl.

Although there is no record of Van Gogh having read the American Transcendentalists, I'm struck by how he and Henry David Thoreau share a common understanding of nature as having an essential unity. The Transcendentalists, influenced by the German philosopher Immanuel Kant, believed the source of this unity was a kind of elixir: Emerson called it the "over-soul." But Thoreau, influenced by the Prussian writer Alexander Von Humboldt, believed this unity could be understood more scientifically, through observation and recording of detail.

Van Gogh seems to have embraced both views, some of his paintings reflecting the smallest detail in a flower or his lover's face, while other paintings explore, through the intensity of color and use of overlapping forms, the energy of the entire universe. If Von Humboldt is our first ecological scientist, perhaps Van Gogh is our first ecological painter; everything he saw is connected to everything else.

Drawing of Bird's Nest

In September 1888, Van Gogh wrote: "If we study Japanese art, we see a man who is undoubtedly wise, philosophic and intelligent, and who spends his time how? In studying the distance between the earth and the moon? No. In studying the policy of Bismarck? No. He studies a single blade of grass, and shows how it is connected to the whole.

Drawing of The Sower (after Millet)

"And we cannot study Japanese art, it seems to me, without becoming much gayer and happier, and without realizing we must return to nature in spite of our education and our work in a world of convention. I envy the Japanese the extreme

Drawing of Cart on Bridge

clearness which everything has in their work. It flows, never is wearisome, never seems to be done too hurriedly. Their work is as simple as breathing, and they draw a figure in a few sure strokes with the same ease as if it were as simple as buttoning a coat ..."

The question of what particular mental illness, or nervous disorder, Van Gogh suffered from is a difficult one. While writing the poems, I asked a psychotherapist if a diagnosis was possible for a dead person, and one who lived years before the DSM, the contemporary manual of diagnostic disorders by which psychiatric patients are categorized in modern medicine.

She told me it did matter if the patient was dead. The purpose of diagnosis is to design helpful treatments, not label dead people.

A popular idea about Van Gogh, based on certain aspects of his behavior—explosive outbursts, bouts of depression, periods of intense artistic activity—is

Drawing of Dr. Gachet

that he must have suffered from Bipolar Disorder. Some psychologists, with limited evidence, have argued that more artists suffer from the highs and lows of this illness than non-artists. I find this to be a romantic misconception based on the assumption that an artist is more productive in the manic phase of the disorder than the depressive one. Full blown mania, however, seems to be characterized more by disorganization and impulsiveness than by productive labor. Van Gogh's productivity—paintings, drawings, and letters—is staggering.

One of the ironies of Van Gogh's life and work is his meeting a "mental doctor"—Dr. Gachet—who also painted. Gachet hospitalized Van Gogh in Auvers and they became friends. Van Gogh observed in a letter to Theo that Gachet "seems to be suffering from the same mental disorder as me"—and then painted Gachet's portrait.

In Paul Gruchow's memoir, *Letters to a Young Madman,* the author devotes an entire page to this ironic juxtaposition in Van Gogh's work: "There are two portraits in Van Gogh's oeuvre that bear uncanny similarities," Gruchow wrote, "one of them painted in 1889, the other in 1890. Both subjects sit at the same angle. They have the same nose, the same eyes, the same chin, the same moustache, the same wing-like tufts of side hair. Their clothes drape in the same manner. They are rendered in similar colors. They have the same doleful and somewhat weary expression. They exude the same air of intensity. If one knew nothing about those paintings, one would say that they are alternative views of the same man, or portraits of brothers. In fact, however, one is a painting of a hospital patient, and the other a portrait of the psychiatrist with whom Van Gogh spent his last days. And there is a difference: Dr. Gachet is portrayed with hands; the insane man isn't.

Sorrow– Drawing of Sein Hoornik

"Van Gogh himself, of course, was the patient in insane asylums and killed himself at the age of 37.

Does his inability to see the difference between one of his fellow inmates and one of his doctors mean that the difference was not visible? Or does it mean that it takes a sane man to see the difference?" (*Letters to a Young Madman,* Paul Gruchow, p. 102)

So then, what caused Van Gogh's madness? Because there is evidence other members of his family suffered from mental disorders, including a sister who spent much of her life in an asylum, there is probably a genetic component to his instability. But my sense is that he also suffered from an inability to mourn the many losses in his life, and from what Alan Wolfelt, an authority in the field of bereavement, has called "the ghosts of grief."

Vincent was named for his brother, Vincent Willem, who was stillborn exactly one year before Vincent the painter. Vincent aspired to become a Protestant minister, his first vocation, and failed. His numerous love affairs were failures, and the most serious of them, with the prostitute Sien Hoornik, was forbidden by his father. His friendship with Gauguin ended with Vincent cutting off his own ear, and their dream of an artist colony in Provence died along with the friendship. Finally, although arguably the greatest painter of modern times, he sold only one painting in his lifetime.

Wolfelt has written about the effects of unmourned loss, and about how normal depression is in the face of loss. "How ironic is it that we try to push away or fend off what is a life-given condition—the need to mourn? Some families have a long-held tradition of responding defensively in the face of life losses.

"For many, the resistance to the pain and

Drawing of Man Crying

discomfort that accompanies loss is passed down from one generation to the next. When family rules do not allow for true feelings, the capacity to mourn is inhibited, delayed, converted, or avoided completely. The family rule, although unwritten and usually unspoken, is often loud and clear: "Thou shall not mourn!" Yet, until you can authentically mourn life losses, you become stuck and are at risk for depression, anxiety and a host of other problems." (Wolfelt, p. 2)

Wolfelt goes on to explain the need for a "safe place" and "safe people" with whom to mourn.

It seems clear from his letters that Van Gogh's safe place was nature, and his most enduring relationship—his friendship with his brother Theo—was his safest human connection, communicating this feeling as early as 1883 in a letter to Theo from The Hague: "I have in fact no other friend but you, and when I am in low spirits, I always think of you. I only wish you were here, that we might consult once more about moving to the country."

Several years later, Vincent would explain to his brother that he was being treated in an asylum because he believed he was being poisoned by local townspeople who had no appreciation for art or artists. One wonders if this was psychotic paranoia or if Van Gogh meant that it was his soul being poisoned, spiritually, by his neighbors' paranoia about Van Gogh.

Whatever he meant, it was Theo alone with whom he shared this traumatic experience. But the geographical distance with his brother, who more

Grave Site of Vincent and Theo Van Gogh

than anyone appreciated his genius and tried valiantly to support him, was never bridged during their lifetime.

Vincent and Theo are buried next to each other in the cemetery in Auvers.

A Note on Method

I'm not aware that I wrote the poems in *Dreaming with Open Eyes* with any particular technique in mind. I'm not a formalist, but writing in shorter lines than I had ever used seemed to help the shape and various voices within the poems, especially Van Gogh's.

The first poems were written in the summer of 2003, which I sent to author Paul Gruchow, who praised them and encouraged me to write more. Paul began, then, to write his memoir, *Letters to a Young Madman*, which explores his experiences with mental illness and the mental health treatment system. We exchanged and critiqued what he called our "parallel" writing, until his tragic suicide in 2004. He loved and identified with Van Gogh and was probably the most brilliant person I've ever known. His validation of those first poems was critical in the development of this book.

During the next fourteen years I wrote the rest of the poems. I did very little revision, waiting for poems to emerge from my study of Van Gogh and from my own evolving understanding of art and artists. I chose to not publish any of the poems until they were all written, perhaps identifying in that way with Van Gogh himself.

Instead of publishing in journals, a process that depends these days on networking, I contacted several art museums and studios, a bookstore, and was contacted by the Mayo Clinic. I told them I was developing a poetry manuscript exploring the life and work of Vincent Van Gogh and asked if I could read and discuss some of it. The response surprised me: I was not turned down, even though the poems had yet to find a publisher interested in issuing the collection.

At an art and antique studio Van Gogh birthday party, in Glendale, Ohio, I was paired with Per Knutson, a restorative arts expert at the Cincinnati Art Museum. I had watched Per restore Van Gogh's iconic masterpiece, *Two Figures in Undergrowth*, at the museum, amazed at how his painstaking removal of preservative wax from the painting brought back Van Gogh's original, brilliant colors and made visible flowers that had disappeared. In a bookstore in Minnesota, someone in the audience told me I had "channeled" Van Gogh, which I took to be a compliment.

At the Mayo Clinic, I was featured at a conference—*The Many Faces of Trauma*—where I read many of these poems to a diverse audience of health professionals. Then I asked them to create a treatment plan for Van Gogh. I was surprised by how many psychiatrists, social workers, chaplains, and other professionals identified Vincent's vocational issues, his career as an unknown painter, as the primary source of his depression and mental instability. Their treatment plans explored ways they might have helped him earn a living and overcome his sense of failure.

My most memorable experience was a social worker in one of these venues who asked me if the poems were personal. Of course the poems are personal. I love Van Gogh's art. It's a source of creative inspiration for me. But also, I lost my father to depression and suicide in 1989. Then in 2004, my friend Paul Gruchow died the same way.

With regard to the title of this book, I'll let Van Gogh have the last word: this, written from Arles in September 1888—"I have a wonderful lucidity at moments, these days when nature is so beautiful, I am not conscious of myself anymore and the painting comes to me as in a dream."

—Louis Martinelli, Cincinnati, Ohio, 2020.

Acknowledgements

Gruchow, Paul. *Letters to a Young Madman*. 2012. Levins Publishing.

Wolfelt, Alan. *Living in The Shadow of The Ghosts of Grief*. 2016. Companion Press.

Van Gogh's Letters—there are over 900 of them—are in the public domain. Most of them were collected after his death by Johanna van Gogh-Bonger, Vincent's sister-in-law. They were published in 1914.

Van Gogh's pen and ink drawings are an important part of his work. Many of them served as studies for his paintings. There are over 1,000 drawings and watercolors and 860 oil paintings. One of the drawings is of Van Gogh's friend, Arles postmaster Joseph Roulin, whose family Vincent painted.

Drawing of The Sower

The Postman, Joseph Roulin

Many people were helpful during this process. I want to thank especially my wife Teresa Dutko, for her support and for helping me understand the role of loss in Van Gogh's life; the artist, Calista Bockenstette, for teaching me so much about art and about Van Gogh; Per Knutson, for sharing with me his restoration of *Two Figures in Undergrowth*, at the Cincinnati Art Museum; Professor Diane McNally

Forsyth for her encouragement and for connecting me to the Mayo Clinic Conference planning committee; Dr. Christian Knoeller, with whom I shared the manuscript and friendship; the late Earl F. Potvin, the first great artist to grace my life, walk miles with me, and share his love of Van Gogh; and Tom Driscoll, Managing editor of Shipwreckt Books, who believed in this project.

Forgive the words of thanks I did not say to teachers Wendell Berry, Michael Dennis Browne and Robert Bly.

Chronology of Van Gogh's Life

1851, May, The Calvinist Minister, Reverend Theodoros van Gogh marries Anna Cornelia Carbentus in Zundert, Holland.

1852, March 30, Birth and death of the first Vincent Willem van Gogh.

1853, March 30, Birth of Vincent Willem van Gogh, the future painter.

1857, Birth of Theo van Gogh.

1864, Vincent attends boarding school.

1869, Begins apprenticeship at his Uncle Cent's art gallery, The Hague.

1873, Lodges at Mrs. Sarah Loyer's house, falls in love with Mrs. Loyer's daughter, is rebuffed, becomes depressed and turns to religion for comfort.

1876-1879, Delivers first sermon as an apprentice "curate." Studies at theological and missionary school. Fails to qualify, moves to southern Belgium, and works as a mission preacher with mining families. He is dismissed for unconventional behavior.

1880, Registers at Royal Academy of Fine Arts to study drawing and painting, Brussels.

1881, Returns to live at his family's parsonage. Falls in love with his cousin, who rejects him. Visits another cousin, the painter Anton Mauve, and spends a month studying with him. After a bitter argument with his father on December 25, Vincent leaves parent's home.

1882, Sets up house with Clasina Maria Hoornik (Sien), a prostitute, and her daughter. He is hospitalized with gonorrhea.

1883, Leaves Hoornik under pressure from his family, concentrates on painting.

1884, Meets neighbor Margot Bergemann, who falls in love with him and attempts suicide.

1885, Vincent's father is buried on Vincent's birthday. Works on painting he calls "The Potato Eaters." Leaves Nuenen in wake of scandals. A local priest has forbidden women to sit for Van Gogh portraits. He is treated for syphilis. Paints the first of many self-portraits.

1886-1888, Moves to Paris to live with his brother Theo and Theo's fiancé. Meets prominent painters, among them Gauguin, Degas, and Pissarro. Vincent exhibits his own work.

1888, Moves to Arles, France with plans to establish an artist's co-operative in Provence. Moves into the Yellow House and Paul Gauguin joins him there. Cuts off lobe of ear and gives it to Rachel, a prostitute at The House of Tolerance. Vincent is hospitalized for mental crisis. Gauguin leaves. Van Gogh enters an asylum.

1890, Theo sells one of Vincent's paintings, "The Red Vines," for 400 francs, the only Van Gogh painting to sell during the artist's lifetime. Vincent moves to Auvers, France, where he works on the portrait of Dr. Gachet, his new "mental doctor." He completes large body of work, including "Two

Figures in Undergrowth." On July 29, two days after shooting himself in the stomach, Van Gogh dies in his brother Theo's arms.

Theo, suffering from syphilis and severe stress, collapses and is admitted to a clinic near Paris where he is certified "insane" and committed to a mental hospital in Holland.

1891, Theo dies from dementia paralytica.

1914, Theo's widow, Johanna van Gogh-Bonger, has Theo's bones transferred to a grave beside Vincent's at Auvers, France.

1978, Theo's son, Vincent, dies at age 88.

About the Poet

Louis Martinelli, poet, playwright, essayist and educator, is a graduate of St. Mary's University and The University of Cincinnati, where he developed innovative educational programs, including a medical ethics curriculum.

Louis has been a Writer in Residence in many Midwestern communities and organizations, including The Mayo Clinic and The Northfield Arts Guild, where he was commissioned to write a series of dramatic monologues about mother-child bonding and loss. The most widely produced of these, *Wild Iris*, has been performed in theatres, medical centers, and conferences in the United States and Europe. His play, *Take My Hand*, won a National Endowment for The Arts outstanding achievement award.

In 2001, Martinelli was nominated for a MacArthur Foundation Award for his work in helping create sustainable communities.

He is literary executor of environmental writer Paul Gruchow's estate as well as founder and director of The Paul Gruchow Foundation.

Up On Big Rock Poetry Series
SHIPWRECKT BOOKS PUBLISHING COMPANY
Minnesota

IN®
DIE

Made in the USA
Monee, IL
15 November 2020

47819314R00069